e Security, Peace, and Prosperity of the Nation of Israel

Seventy Years of Miracles

www.HolyLandGifts.net

Publisher and Marketing—Zvi Zachor

Editor—John D. Garr, Ph.D.

Concept and Art Design—Michael Amar

ISBN: 978-0-9962647-2-3

Table of Contents

ISRAEL

The Nation of Miracles

The 1948 Declaration of the Establishment of the State of Israel represented one of the greatest miracles in human history. The Jewish people, whose nation had been destroyed nearly two thousand years earlier, were finally restored to their ancestral homeland. Then, their nation was revived just as God had promised through the prophet Isaiah as a nation "born in one day"—on May 14, 1948. The centuries of emotional and physical pain that the Jews had suffered at the hands of emperors, kings, dictators, and prelates was turned into joy. As King David had predicted, the God of Israel "turned [their] mourning into dancing!" A new nation had emerged from the ashes of history's darkest and deadliest event, the Holocaust, and Israel began a miracle-filled transformation into a beacon of freedom, prosperity, and hope for enduring peace.

David Ben-Gurion, Israel's first prime minister, said it well: "In Israel, in order to be a realist you must believe in miracles!" The reality is that Israel's very existence in defiance of all the laws of history for the assimilation of conquered peoples is a miracle; however, Israel's continued development in the midst of an often hostile and violent area is a continuing, day-to-day miracle. Despite unrelenting assaults by contentious neighbors on its citizens and its sovereignty, Israel has continued not only to survive but also to thrive for seventy years now.

The degree of safety and security that has made the growth and development of Israel possible has been secured and maintained largely by the Israel Defense Forces (IDF). In the memorable Six-Day War in 1967, the IDF succeeded in stopping a planned invasion by its Arab neighbors when it launched a preemptive strike that defeated Israel's enemies and liberated Judea and Samaria—including Jerusalem and the Temple Mount—from foreign occupation. The Israeli Air Force defended the sovereignty and security of Israel in a metaphorical fulfillment of Isaiah's memorable words, "As birds flying, so will the Lord of hosts defend Jerusalem."

From being a largely abandoned and inhospitable land of deserts and swamps only two centuries ago, Israel has become perhaps the most amazing agricultural wonder of the world. The Israeli people have literally caused "the desert to bloom as a crocus," the miracle that Isaiah also predicted. The genius of Israeli agronomists and the tireless work of *kibbutzim* and other agricultural enterprises have produced a miraculous transformation of the land itself. Israel's stunning development of drip-irrigation technology has set the world's gold standard for making desert land productive. Israel has also become a world leader in horticulture and genetic agriculture. Israeli agriculture provides an abundance of food which feeds the nation's seven million citizens and is also distributed around the world.

In less than seventy years, the tiny nation of Israel has also become a world leader in science and technology. Israel now ranks first in the world in recycled water technology and application, and it has developed the science of desalinization of sea water to provide quality drinking water for its citizens. Israel has also become a world leader in sustainable energy development. Amazing achievements in the technology of unmanned aerial vehicles and driverless automobiles have been made in Israel. Israel has become a world leader in scientific development to such a degree that all major technology companies in the world—including IBM, Microsoft, Apple, and Google—have research laboratories in Israel. It is no surprise that six living Nobel Prize winners are Israeli citizens! Many of the electronic wonders of the modern world were invented in Israel by Israeli citizens.

The reality is this: Israel's very existence is a miracle, and its continuing existence as a vibrant, thriving nation despite living under the constant threat of violence from terrorist neighbors and antisemitic world powers abroad is a continuing day-by-day miracle.

GPO/Kobi Gideon

The Knesset, Israel's National Legislature

Preparing the Way for Restoring the Nation of Israel

Prayers at the Western Wall

In the eighteenth century, the Jewish people who had long been evicted and banished from their ancestral homeland began to make *aliyah* by going up to Israel and its capital city of Jerusalem. These Jews assumed enormous risks when they listened to their hearts' cry to fulfill the dream that their ancestors had had for nearly 2,000 years: to return to their land, possess it, and build a nation of freedom and security for themselves and their children.

The bravery and vigor of these Jewish pioneers of restoration finally coalesced into The Zionist Movement to produce one of history's most amazing "miracles": the full restoration of the long-dormant nation and land of Israel. In 1897, Jewish journalist Theodore Herzl organized the First Zionist Congress in Basel, Switzerland, with 200 participants from seventeen nations. From its inception, the Zionist movement began to encourage Jewish migration to Israel, and thousands of Jews from around the world responded. Amazing, seemingly miraculous events would follow in the context of Herzl's vision.

Theodore Herzl GPO

The First Zionist Congress, August, 1897

In England, the Balfour Declaration was issued, a document which formalized the need for the restoration of the Jewish state in Palestine. Then, in 1922, the League of Nations unanimously created a Covenant for Palestine that mandated to Britain the responsibility for establishing a Jewish state in Palestine in all of the land west of the Jordan River. Under the authority of the British Mandate, the *Haganah* ("Defense") was formed as a Jewish paramilitary organization that eventually became the Israel Defense Forces (IDF). Then, the White Paper of 1939 was prepared by the British government calling for the establishment of a Jewish national homeland within ten years. The stage was being set for the full restoration of the ancient nation of Israel in the land of Israel.

General Allenby at Jerusalem's Jaffa Gate

Lord Balfour Visiting Tel Aviv

A Mass Demonstration Against the "White Paper Policy"

British Soldiers in the Jewish Quarter of the Old City of Jerusalem

GPO/Matson Eric

1939–1945
War and Holocaust, Israel's Greatest Challenge

Women, Children Surrender to Nazis

Yad vashem

Jews Wearing Yellow Star of David Marked for Death

Yad vashem

Jews Escaping to Israel's Shores

GPO/Pinn Hans

For decades, thousands of Jews had made *aliyah* to their ancestral homeland in preparation for the establishment of the restored nation of Israel; however, the inexorable progress toward their realization of the centuries-old Jewish dream came to a grinding halt in 1939 with the German-initiated World War. Millions of Jews were trapped in Europe when the Allied nations completely stopped their immigration not only into Britain and the United States but also into Palestine.

For six horrible years, the Jewish population of Europe became prey for the German Nazi regime as Adolph Hitler systematically and viciously pursued his lifelong dream to make Europe *judenrein* ("clean of Jews") by orchestrating the genocide of European Jewry. In time, the Nazis would construct well-designed death camps in Eastern Europe which were nothing more than killing machines. There they methodically murdered Jewish men, women, and children with their Zyklon B cyanide gas and then incinerated their bodies in crematoria. The most infamous of these was Auschwitz, where over a million Jews were killed between 1942 and 1944.

By the time that the Allied forces had defeated the German armies, six million Jews, including over one million children, had been murdered in history's most vile example of human depravity. Never before had a people been herded together from across national boundaries and slaughtered simply because of their ethnicity and their religious faith. The Holocaust was, indeed, the greatest tragedy in Jewish history and the greatest atrocity in human history.

World War II confirmed the absolute necessity for the creation of a safe haven where the Jewish people could have complete self-determination, free from political, social, economic, and religious coercion, intimidation, or persecution. So, the Jewish people rose up from the ashes of the Holocaust and resolved to restore their own nation in their own land.

Jewish and Polish Partisans in the Janowa Forest

Hannah Szenes on the Kibbutz

Jewish pilots in World War II

Dancing the Hora in a Tent Camp

1945–1948
Setting the Stage for a Restored Israel

Declaration of the Partition of Israel in the United Nations 1947

The year 1948 was the culmination of more than two centuries of concentrated effort by thousands of faithful and dedicated Jews to restore the Jewish nation to the Jewish people. What had begun as a trickle of Jews who made *aliyah* by "going up" to the land of their ancestors finally resulted a flood of those who responded to the inner voice that called them irresistibly to their destiny by returning to the land that had always been rightfully theirs. This restoration produced the miraculous restoration of Israel—the people, the nation, and the land.

The dangerous and laborious tasks of reclaiming deserts, swamps, and wastelands that those Jewish pioneers had undertaken came to fruition on May 14, 1948 when David Ben-Gurion issued the Declaration of the Establishment of the State of Israel that formalized the creation of the new, yet ancient, nation. As the prophet had predicted, Israel was miraculously "born in one day," just as it had been 3,500 years before at Sinai. The labors of thousands of Jews over two centuries produced the miracle of the twentieth century—an event that the Jewish people had long expected but had thought virtually impossible since the time of the Roman occupation of ancient Israel and the eviction and dispersion of their ancestors. The ancient nation of Israel was resurrected to stand again in the same land in which it had been originally established.

A Parade of Joy over the Partition Declaration

Dancing the Hora in a Kibbutz

GPO/Kluger Z

IDF Soldiers in Folk Dance

Men and Women Stand Guard

Early Desert Agriculture

Immigrants from Yemen Celebrate Passover in Israel

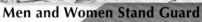

11

1948

The Re-Establishment of the Nation of Israel

Though the Jewish people who had returned to their land were surrounded by the armies of hostile nations that sought their destruction, they succeeded in reestablishing their own nation, a land dedicated to peace, justice, and good will, on the very soil that God had given irrevocably to Abraham, their ancient patriarch, forever. This was the place where the one and only God had chosen to place his name, and that ancient holy land was reclaimed and rededicated to the divine precepts of *shalom* (peace), *chesed* (loving-kindness), and *tzedakah* (justice).

The capital of the new Israel was Jerusalem, the same city that the Jewish people had revered from the time of Abraham. The government for the Chosen People was established in the same place where the palaces of King David and King Solomon once stood and where the Holy Temple was situated two millennia ago. *Yerushalayim* (Jerusalem) had always stood for peace, for its very name means "foundation of peace." The restored Jerusalem merely continued the Jewish expectation for lasting peace that would one day encompass the globe. Through the past 70 years, the Israeli people have maintained the tradition of praying and working for peace.

The signing of the Declaration of the Establishment of the State of Israel set in motion the process by which a largely inhospitable land would gradually blossom as the rose and become the agricultural wonder of the world. It also set in motion the development of a strong democratic state—the first such state in the history of the Middle East and its only free nation. This action 70 years ago made it posible for the Jewish people, who had endured nearly two millennia of persecution and violence, to build a place of social, political, and military security where they could control their own destiny.

GPO/Kluger Zolfan

David Ben Gurion Declares Israel's Statehood

IDF archives

General Moshe Dayan Leads War with Egypt

Haganah archives

A new nation, a new people, a new land came to life from the remnants of an ancient nation, an ancient people, and an ancient land. *Am Yisrael Chai* (the People of Israel life)! And the nation, people, and land now thrive as never before in the history of the Jewish people. Now, that's a miracle!

Women and Men Share the Battle

David Ben Gurion Studies War Maps

The Battle Rages in the South

Famous "Ink Flag" Hoisted in Eilat

1948–1955
Securing and Building the New Israel

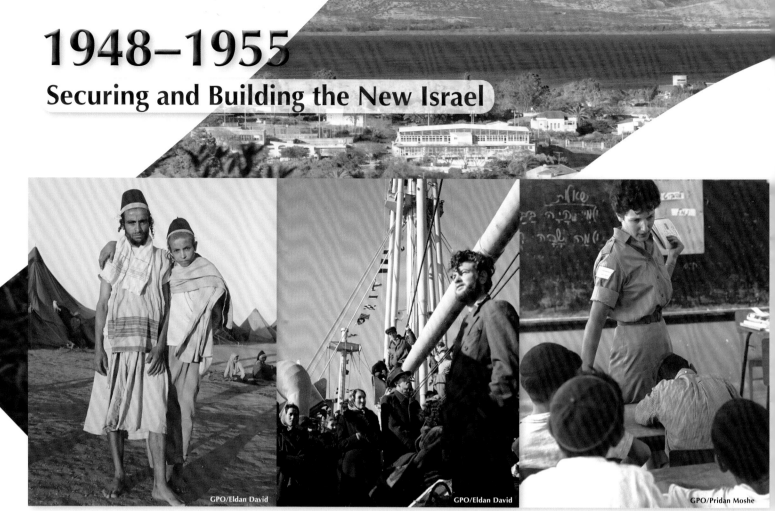

Yemenite Jews Making Aliyah — GPO/Eldan David

Immigrants Disembarking from Ship — GPO/Eldan David

Israeli Educators Teaching Children — GPO/Pridan Moshe

Ships Teeming with Jewish Immigrants Making Aliyah to Israel

In 1948, the birth of the new nation of Israel was followed by a massive exodus of Jews from Europe and from Arab and Muslim nations into their ancestral homeland. Just as the prophet Jeremiah predicted, this regathering of the "exiles of Israel" from all the countries to which they were banished surely eclipsed even the magnitude and miracles of the Exodus from Egypt! By 1951, the Jewish population of Israel had doubled its total in 1948 as more than 700,000 Jews from all across the world streamed into the newly restored sovereign nation.

When it was established in 1948, the new nation of Israel became the first democracy in the Middle East with a 120-seat parliament, the Knesset, members of which were first elected in January, 1940. David Ben-Gurion was appointed as Israel's first Prime Minister. The Knesset also elected Chaim Weitzmann the first President of Israel. The parliamentary democracy in Israel has ensured that all Israeli citizens have a voice in the affairs of state.

Picking Fruit in Kibbutz

Many of the immigrants who made *aliyah* to Israel were Holocaust survivors. Because most were indigent, they endured an Austerity Period in which food, clothing, and other necessities were rationed. One of the programs that had been instituted that helped advance the fledgling nation's economy were the *kibbutzim*, cooperatives that led Israel's inventive agricultural revolution that has since become the envy of the world.

In 1950 the Knesset passed the Law of Return which ensured that all people of Jewish ancestry had the right to return to Israel and gain citizenship. In that year, some 50,000 Yemenite Jews were brought to Israel on secret flights. Similar exercises brought Jews from most nations of northern Africa. By 1955, the population had more than doubled again to two million! Israel was well on its way to prosperity.

Celebrating with Dance in Kibbutz Ein Harod

Building Roads the Old Fashioned Way!

GPO/Brauner Teddy

1955–1967
Accelerated Growth and Development

Nahalal Moshav, A Stunning Agricultural Cooperative in the Jezreel Valley

GPO/Kluger Zoltan

Working in the Factories of Israel

GPO/Herman Channia

Political intrigue among the Arab nation of Northern Africa and Western Europe continued to make the progress of the new nation of Israel difficult. In 1956 Egyptian President Nasser nationalize the British and French-owned Suez Cana and blockaded the Gulf of Aqaba, thereb preventing Israeli access to the Red Sea. military conflict ensued that involved th Israeli Defense Forces and the British an French against Egypt; however, the Unite Nations intervened, demanding a ceasefir which resulted in the first ever dispatch c a UN "Emergency Force," a peacekeepin effort. The controversy between Israel an Egypt continued to fester throughout thi period, and drums of war continued t bring threats to the peace and security c Israel.

Despite the hostility of its Arab neighbors the Israeli people continued to strive an thrive. More and more Holocaust survivor were welcomed to the nation as they le the nations where they had endured grea suffering under the German Nazi regime Israeli agriculture continued to make th desert bloom as a crocus as Isaiah ha predicted. Innovative means of irrigatio were developed to make this proces viable and prosperous. Low-tech industr continued to grow and prosper acros the land, providing employment for th continuing stream of Jews who had mad *aliyah* to their ancestral homeland. Th steady growth and relative tranquility wa led by Prime Minister David Ben-Gurio who had announced the independence c the nation of Israel in 1948.

Building Structures in the Desert

GPO/Kluger Z

In 1960, one of the top officials in the Nazi Holocaust, Adolf Eichmann, was brought to justice for his war crimes. The Eichmann trial created worldwide publicity that led to expanded public awareness of the Holocaust and a commitment by many non-Jewish nations to join the Israeli people in the declaration, "Never again!"

Trial of Nazi War Criminal Adolph Eichmann

The Invention of the Uzi Machine Gun

Soldiers Vote for the First Knesset (Parliament)
GPO/Mendelson Hugo

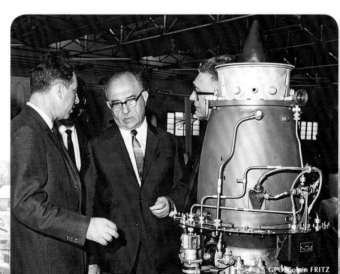

Prime Minister Levi Eshkol and Defense Minister Shimon Peres at a Jet Engine Manufacturing Plant

Victory Parade as Thousands Watch and Cheer

GPO/Eldan David

1967

The Restoration of Jerusalem and the Temple Mount

The year 1967 was absolutely pivotal in the development of the nation of Israel. Immediately after the Declaration of the Establishment of the State of Israel in 1948, Israel had been attacked by all of the hostile neighbors that surrounded them. While the Israel Defense Forces (IDF) had been able to repel most of those attacks, they were unable to drive the armies of Jordan from parts of Jerusalem, including the Temple Mount, and from Judea and Samaria (the land that is often called the West Bank). The overall scene of violence against Israel continued until 1967, when the same hostile forces that had attacked the nation in 1948 arrayed themselves for yet another war which they were sure would totally destroy the nation of Israel.

In early 1967, the leaders of the Arab and Muslim nations that surrounded Israel began to threaten the very existence of the Jewish people. Egypt's president, Gamal Abdel Nasser blocked he Straits of Tiran, closing Israel's access to the Red Sea through the port of Eilat. Then, on May 27, Nasser boasted, "We intend to open a general assault against Israel. . . . Our basic aim will be to destroy Israel." King Faisal of Saudi Arabia declared, "The Arab nations should sacrifice up to 10 million of their 50 million people, if necessary to wipe out Israel."

Believing that the leaders of the Arab nations meant precisely what they had said, Israel wisely initiated a preemptive attack on Egypt on June 5, 1967, in which the Israeli Air Force destroyed more than three hundred Egyptian airplanes on the ground, and the Israeli Defense Force subsequently routed the Egyptian army of 100,000 in the Sinai Peninsula. At that time, Jordan joined the attack on Israel. The Jordanian efforts were repelled by the IDF, giving Israel an opportunity to liberate Jerusalem, Judea, and Samaria, the land that Jordan had illegally occupied since 1948 when King Abdullah had invaded Jerusalem and the West Bank. The IDF also repelled the Syrian Armies and secured the Golan Heights, thereby bringing to an end the periodic and indiscriminate Arab shelling of the greater Galilee.

The Heat of the Battle in Sinai

81X972

IDF archiv

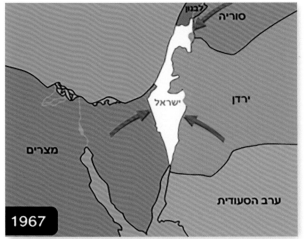

The Three-Pronged Arab Offensive, Six-Day War

Column of Military Vehicles Headed for Battle

Preparing to Liberate the Temple Mount

Levi Eshkol, Prime Minister of Israel

Israeli Paratroopers Preparing to Go to Battle in Sinai

GPO/Yaacov Agor

1967
The Restoration of Jerusalem and the Temple Mount

Entering the Gates of Jerusalem

GPO/Ilan Bruner

The war that was expected to destroy Israel became one of Israel's greatest triumphs and came to be called the "Six-Day War." Amazingly, the IDF defeated the Egyptian armies, liberated Jerusalem and the Temple Mount, along with the rest of Judea and Samaria, from Jordanian occupation, and seized control of the Golan Heights from Syria, bringing security to the northern Galilee. Finally, after nearly 2,000 years of foreign occupation, Israelis and Jews around the world were able to pray at their holiest shrine, the Western Wall of the Temple Mount! What a miracle and testimony to God's faithfulness.

The Six-Day War radically altered the Arab-Israeli conflict, for by liberating the West Bank from Jordanian occupation and taking the Golan Heights from Syria, the IDF established greater security for the citizens of Israel. Israel's major population centers, industrial assets, and military bases were no longer easy targets for Arab armies and terrorist organizations. The Jewish people, who had been vulnerable to terrorist attacks and to the threats of their Muslim neighbors, achieved much greater security and peace through this military action.

Liberating the Holy City from Arab Occupation

GPO/Ilan Brur

The Six-Day War seemed miraculous to many Israelis as many events on the battlefields were so unusual that they could have been seen as involving divine intervention. Israel's enemies were utterly defeated, the Temple Mount was liberated so that Jews once again could pray at the site of the Holy Temple, and the nation as a whole was infinitely more secure.

Celebrating Liberty at the Western Wall

In Awe at the Western Wall of the Temple

In the Thick of the Battle to Secure Freedom of All Israel

Soldiers Pray at the Liberated Western Wall

IDF archives

Growing Aliyah and Economic Development

Israel's Prime Minister Gold Meir

Optics Research Laboratory

GPO/Eldan David

GPO/Milner

New Immigrants Learn Hebrew

GPO/Sa'ar Ya

After the Six-Day War and the improvement of the security of Israel against attacks from its neighbors and the Muslim terrorists—including suicide bombers—that had inflicted death upon Israeli civilians for decades, increasing numbers of Jews from around the world began to make *aliyah* to their land. These included significant numbers from the Soviet Union after the ban on Jewish emigration from Russia and other Eastern European nations was finally lifted in 1971. Thousands of famous *Refusniks* who were illegitimately detained in Russia undertook *aliyah* to Israel where they were welcomed.

During this time, Israeli citizens undertook efforts to reclaim Judea and Samaria by constructing settlements in the land that had been illegally occupied by the Jordanian armies in 1948 and liberated in the Six-Day War. The so-called "West Bank" has always been and will continue to be a part of Israel, the land that God conveyed to Abraham and his descendants forever. Efforts were also made to secure the Golan Heights which the IDF had conquered from Syria after its invasion of northern Israel.

After Israel liberated Jerusalem and the Temple Mount from Jordanian occupation in 1967, access to the Western Wall, Judaism's holiest site, was secured and granted to all Jewish people, both Israeli citizens and those from around the world. In the true spirit of religious liberty, the site was opened to all people of all faiths (in contrast to its being closed to anyone but Muslims during the Jordanian occupation).

In 1969, Golda Meir was elected Prime Minister of Israel, becoming the first woman to lead a Middle Eastern nation since biblical times. Meir remained in this position until 1974, leading the nation in efforts toward peace, and presiding over prosperity despite the continuing efforts by Israel's neighbors to foment conflict and turmoil.

Electronics Factory in Ashkelon

GPO/Cohen Fritz

Celebrating Shavuot

GPO/Kluger Zoltan

GPO/Moshe Milner

New Settlement in Hafa Bayt

GPO/Kluger Zoltan

1973
The Yom Kippur War—Overcoming Yet Another Challenge

Helicopter Rescue

GPO/Ron Ilan

GPO/David Ru

Chief of Staff David Elazar Leading the Battle

Evangelist Billy Graham and
U. S. President Richard Nixon

IDF Soldiers in the Heat of Battle

GPO/Spector Ze'ev

On October 6, 1973, Israel's hostile Syrian and Egyptian neighbors launched an insidious surprise attack against Israel on the holiest day of the Jewish religious calendar, *Yom Kippur*, the Day of Atonement when all adult Jews are required by the Torah to fast and engage in acts of repentance. Early on in this invasion, many doubted whether the Israeli Defense Forces (IDF) would be able to prevail against this attack; however, the United States, along with the Soviet Union, rushed arms to its ally Israel.

Amazingly—if not miraculously—the Syrian army was repulsed in the Golan Heights by a small remnant of an Israeli tank force and driven out of not only Israel but also the Golan. Then, the IDF fiercely fought the Egyptians, crossing the Suez Canal and trapping the Egyptian Third Army only 50 miles from Cairo. Had it not been for the massive air delivery of arms and supplies that were airlifted from the United States, however, the story could well have been much different. It was reported that famed Christian minister Dr. Billy Graham, intervened directly with U. S. President Richard Nixon to come to Israel's rescue by supplying what Israel needed to avoid disaster.

The surprise invasion of the Syrian and Egyptian armies cost the lives of some 2,000 Israeli soldiers and pointed out Israel's vulnerability to such invasions. Consequently, the Israeli government initiated efforts to increase its military preparedness for the defense of the nation in the event that its hostile neighbors chose to launch additional surprise attacks upon them in the future. This led to the strengthening of the IDF that has continually protected the sovereignty of the nation of Israel and the security of its people.

Generals in the Heat of the Battle

Soldiers Pause for Prayer

Tanks Crossing the Suez Canal into Egypt

1973–1976
Protecting Israeli Citizens, Rescuing Hostages from Entebbe

As a result of the defeat of the Syrian and Egyptian armies in the *Yom Kippur* War, Saudi Arabia initiated an oil embargo against countries that traded with Israel, causing many nations to discontinue their relations with Israel. Even though Syria and Egypt were the aggressors in the war, Israel was blamed and punished by the world community. A time of economic hardship ensued in which the people of Israel suffered considerably because of the efforts of Western nations to protect their own interests at the expense of Israel.

In 1976, an Air France aircraft was hijacked by 40 Palestinian terrorists and flown to Uganda. When the terrorists threatened to kill all the more than 100 Jewish passengers, Israeli Prime Minister Yitzak Rabin ordered Operation Thunderbolt, which became known as the Entebbe Operation, in a bold action that freed the Jewish hostages. This daring operation lasted only 90 minutes, during which all of the hijackers were killed, Uganda's air force was destroyed, and the Jews, with the exception of two who died in the fighting, were freed. In response, United Nations Secretary General Kurt Waldheim, a former Nazi and suspected war criminal, condemned the raid as a "serious violation of the national sovereignty of a United Nations member state," hollow words that the Israeli government ignored.

General Avigdor Kahalani in the Golan Heights

Battles in the Golan Heights

Celebrating Victory, Waving Israeli Flag

In spite of yet another effort to destroy Israel and bring about the genocide of the Jewish people, the Israelis were victorious against the military might of its neighbors. Though times were economically difficult, the nation continued not only to survive, but also to grow in number as Jews from around the world continued to stream into Israel to claim their rightful patrimony, the land and nation of their ancestors. The drums of war could not drown out the spirit of the Jewish people and their determination to live and prosper in their ancestral homeland.

Rescued Hostages Disembarking from Airplanes in Israel

Lt. Col. Jonathan Netanyahu Leads Rescue Mission

1976–1978
Peace Agreements and Greater Security

Prime Minister Menachem Begin and
U. S. President Jimmy Carter

Prime Minister Yitzhak Rabin and
U. S. President Gerald Ford

GPO/Sa'ar Ya'acov

Egyptian President Anwar Sadat, U.S. President Jimmy Carter, and Israeli Prime Minister Menachem Begin

GPO/Sa'ar Ya'acov

GPO/Pridan Moshe

ctory Workers Constructing Israeli Aircraft

In 1977, Menachem Begin became the first conservative Prime Minister of Israel. Under Begin's leadership, a rapprochement with Egypt developed which resulted in Egyptian President Anwar Sadat's bold effort to bring an end to thirty years of hostility between Egypt and Israel. At Begin's invitation, Sadat visited Jerusalem for two days of talks that included a speech before the Knesset. In making this bold move, Begin and Sadat together changed the corporate psychologies of their nations—and the entire Middle East, for that matter—creating the hope that peace might even be possible. For the first time in centuries of Muslim hegemony over Israel (Palestine) and then of continual Muslim attacks upon the Jewish people after the formation of the nation of Israel in 1948, the Egyptian leader formally recognized the right of Israel to exist, and he and Begin established a foundation for peace negotiations between their nations.

In September, 1978, United States President Jimmy Carter invited Sadat and Begin to come to the U.S. for a peace conference which resulted in the Camp David accords that a framework for negotiating peace in the Middle East. Then, on March 26, 1979, Menachem Begin and Anwar Sadat signed a formal Peace Treaty that has produced an enduring peaceful relationship between Egypt and the nation of Israel.

Because of the impact of the Saudi Arabian oil embargo on the international community after the 1973 *Yom Kippur* War, extensive pressure was brought to bear on the Middle Eastern nations to forge a peace agreement that might forestall future conflicts. In 1974, Yitzhak Rabin, the man who had shaped and organized Israel's defense forces in the years before the 1967 Six-Day War, became Prime Minister of Israel, the youngest person and the first native-born Israeli citizen to serve in that position.

Egyptian President Anwar Sadat Speaks in the Israeli Knesset

GPO/Sa'ar Ya'acov

1982–1990
Wars, Security, and Growth

GPO/Sa'ar Ya'acov

Tanks ready for battle outside Beirut

GPO/Sa'ar Ya'acov

Chief of staff, Raphael Eitan

GPO/Sa'ar Ya'acov

Soldiers in the Heat of the Battle

In 1982, Israel was forced to launch a military action against Lebanon in which the Israel Defense Forces occupied the capital of Beirut because of the actions in Lebanon of Yasser Arafat's Palestinian Liberation Organization, one of history's most insidious terrorist organizations. After this action, the PLO was forced to evacuate from Lebanon to Tunisia. When Israel withdrew its forces to the south of Lebanon, however, another terrorist organization called Hezbollah gained in strength and became a significant and continuing antagonist against the people of Northern Israel.

By 1985, the Israeli economy was suffering inflation at a staggering rate of 480% per year. The government of Prime Minister Shimon Peres instituted price controls, slashed government expenditures, and replaced the old Israel shekel with the New Shekel in order to deal with the situation and its pressure on Israeli citizens. Reasons for this situation that brought economic hardship were complex, including the immigration of indigent Jews from Eastern Europe and the continuing demands for maintaining the security of the nation in the face of growing tensions with its neighbors.

Tank Column Moving to Battle

GPO

In 1990, Israel became the target of terror from the skies after the United States launched the Gulf War against Iraq in response to Iraqi President Saddam Hussein's invasion of Kuwait. Hussein's response was to attack Israel with some 39 Scud missiles. Terror rained from the skies across Israel, especially in Tel Aviv. Eventually, the United States approved the deployment of its Patriot missile defense system to protect Israel from the Scuds.

In spite of the difficult times of hyperinflation and attacks from hostile Arab neighbors and terrorists of various sorts, the will of the Israeli people continued to impel them toward providing for the common defense of all Israel and the welcoming of immigrants to their homeland.

Anti-Missile Missile Battery in Tel Aviv

Chief of Staff Dan Shomron Shakes Hands with the Commander of a Patriot Missile Battery

Missile Defense over Tel Aviv

President Shimon Peres in New Israeli Fighter Jet

31

1991–1995
Terrorism, Aliyah, Settlements, and "Peace" Accords

GPO/IsraelTsvika

Ethiopian Jews Arriving in Tel Aviv

During these years, the Israeli populace continued to grow with Jews from across the world making aliyah to Israel. On May 24–25, 1991, such an effort took place through the amazing covert Israel Defense Forces' airlift of 15,000 Ethiopian "Beta Israel" Jews to Israel—all in the space of 36 hours, relocating these displaced Jews whom history had virtually forgotten to their homeland. This effort represented the Israeli government's commitment to all Jews around the world who choose to immigrate to Israel under the Law of Return.

On September 13, 1993, Israel and the Palestine Liberation Organization agreed to the Oslo Accords which related to transfer of Israeli authority over the "West Bank" (Judea and Samaria) to a Palestinian Authority in an effort to establish a modicum of peace and bring the constant terrorism of the PLO to an end. In 1994, the PLO signed the Gaza-Jericho Agreement, and then later in that year, both the Palestinians and Israel signed the Washington Declaration, which promised a cessation of hostilities. These agreements permitted the PLO to relocate in territories of Gaza and the West Bank and granted a degree of autonomy to the Palestinians. As usual, the Israeli people were willing to sacrifice their own self-interest for the sake of peace—in this case a "peace" that did not long endure.

Prime Minister Rabin Signing Peace Accords

GPO/Avi Ohayon

As the nation endured the mood swings of the Arabs and Palestinians between expressions of bellicosity and peace, the nation continued to grow in number and in economic and social strength. Settlements began to spring up in various parts of Judea and Samaria from which Jews had been restricted for the nineteen years before the Six-Day War. Israel's posture in the international community grew because of its strength and its position as the only democracy in the Middle East.

Bombed Out City Bus Destroyed by Terrorists

Medical Research and Development

Camps for Settlers in Judea and Samaria

Rainbow over New Settlement at Ma'aleh Adumim

1995

The Assassination of Prime Minister Yitzhak Rabin

Israeli Prime Minister Yitzhak Rabin

GPO/Sa'ar Ya'acov

In all of the history of the nation of Israel, one of the greatest tragedies for the Israeli people was the assassination of Prime Minister Yitzhak Rabin in 1995. This event was an absolute shock to the body politic of the nation and to the sensibilities of virtually all Jews around the world. It seemed impossible that in a nation that has always been dedicated to the sanctity of all human life and the free expression of political, sociological, and religious discourse, a young Israeli, who was part of a far-right-wing religious anti-Zionist organization that opposed peace initiatives of the Israeli government, would even dare to take the life of the leader of all Israel because of differences in ideology. This was especially true when viewed in the light of Prime Minister Rabin's career as a hero warrior, defender of the nation.

Joining the military as a teenager, Rabin had served the nation for 27 years with great distinction. As the Chief of the General Staff, he oversaw the Israel Defense Force's stunning victory in the 1967 Six-Day War. Then, after being elected Prime Minister in 1974, he signed the Sinai Interim Agreement and ordered the hostage rescue mission in Entebbe. For many years, he had engaged in extensive peace efforts, negotiating the Oslo Accords in 1993, and being a major factor in and signatory of he Israeli-Palestinian Interim Agreement in 1995, which had promised peaceful relations with the Palestinian Arab community. For all of his efforts toward peace, Rabin had been awarded the Nobel Peace Prize in 1974.

A shocked nation joined in mourning for one of Israel's finest military leaders and one if its best negotiators for peace. A national memorial day has been established on the Israeli calendar to mark the day of Yitzhak Rabin's death.

United States President Bill Clinton

Yitzhak Rabin Receives the Nobel Peace Prize

President Peres on Memorial Day to Yitzhak Rabin

1996–2000
Technological Revolution, Nationwide Growth

Prime Minister Benjamin Netanyahu

In 1996, Benjamin Netanyahu became the prime minister of Israel. In January, 1997, Netanyahu signed the Hebron Protocol with the Palestinian Authority, which was a hope of land for peace. Then, in 1999, Ehud Barak became prime minister and began to withdraw Israeli forces from Lebanon. As a result, Israel became a member of the Western European and Others Group at the United Nations, a position that accorded the Israeli government the right of membership on the Security Council and appointments to the International Court.

During this time, Israel became the startup nation with dramatic changes in economic development that have been widely acknowledged as nothing less than an economic miracle. In 1996 alone, Israeli startups raised $4.8 billion to fund the ventures of new businesses. The nation's desert agriculture became a global model, and its metamorphosis into a high-tech superpower has become one of the greatest success stories in Israeli history. Israel came to have more Nasdaq-listed companies than any other nation in the world with the exception of the United States and China! At the same time, Israel witnessed significant population growth in Jerusalem and across the nation.

Benjamin Netanyahu Meets with Yasser Arafat

Missile Defense System in Action

Computer Science Researchers in Action

GPO/Micha Kirshner

Prime Minister Ehud Barak

GPO/Ifi Ben Ya'acov

GPO/Harnik Nati

Israel Defense Forces Disengagement from Southern Lebanon

Amdocs High-Tech Factory in Ramat Aviv

1996–2000
Technological Revolution, Nationwide Growth

New Immigrants from the Soviet Union

Research and Development

Israeli Fruit Production

Runners Pass David's Citadel at the Old City of Jerusalem

The Christian presence and its support for Israel also increased with the opening of the International Christian Embassy Jerusalem. Other organizations continued to promote Christian involvement in shaping views on Israel in much of the Western world, particularly in the United States.

During this period, many spectacular and noteworthy archaeological discoveries were made in various parts of Israel that continued to connect modern Israel with its historical past and further solidify the right of the Jewish people to inhabit their ancestral homeland.

The people of Israel continue to expand their expectations to become a world leader in science and technology and in the prospects for global peace.

Christians Gather in Jerusalem to Celebrate Israel

Pilgrims in The Church of Mount Tabor

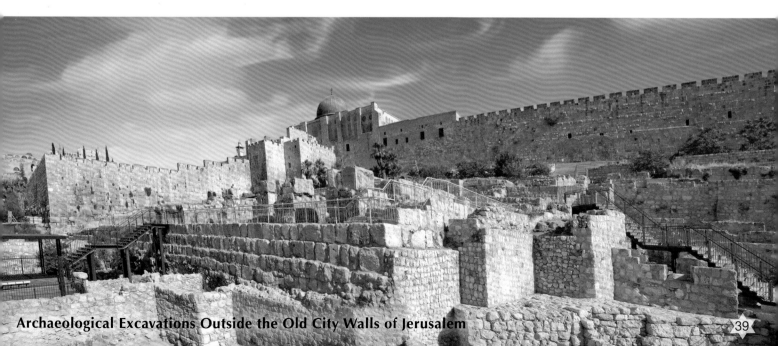

Archaeological Excavations Outside the Old City Walls of Jerusalem

2001–2010
Peace, Missile Defense, Amazing Technology

Prime Minister Ariel Sharon

GPO/Avi Ohayon

During the first decade of the new century, Israel accelerated its commitment to peace and security in the nation for all of its citizens. Despite the failure of previous peace processes, Israel continued to work and to make sacrifices toward achieving a lasting peace. Because of the continuing bellicosity of the Palestinian people in Gaza and the West Bank, many Israelis sought to disengage from them. In 2002, Prime Minister Ariel Sharon launched Operation Defensive Shield to make Israel more secure by constructing a security barrier between it and the West Bank.

In 2005, all Israelis who had settled in Gaza were evacuated and Israel ceded control of Gaza to the Palestinians in hopes of resolving the continuing crises that were regularly created by indiscriminate cross-border attacks by the Muslim terrorist group Hamas. This land-for-peace initiative was doomed to failure, however, because of Palestinian belligerency. Hamas seized control of Gaza in 2007 and, for all intents and purposes, turned it into a fortified center for terror that has continued to afflict Israel to this day.

Ariel Sharon Celebrating Sukkot with Soldiers

Exhibition of Genetically Modified Vegetables
GPO/Mark Neyman

Israeli Research Technology Laboratory
GPO/Avi Oh

Prime Minister Sharon was succeeded as prime minister by Ehud Olmert in 2006. Shortly before that time, Mahmoud Ahmadinejad became president of Iran and immediately began to support Hezbollah in Lebanon and Hamas in Gaza in an effort to foment terror attacks against Israel. Despite the fact of Israeli withdrawal from South Lebanon and Gaza, both of these terrorist organizations, with the support of Iran, have continued to attack Israel, targeting civilian population centers. Israel, in turn, has been forced to launch counterattacks in order to protect its citizens from these indiscriminate acts of terror. The threats from Iran have made it perhaps the greatest existential threat to the nation of Israel as it has fomented terror and violence in most of the countries surrounding Israel as it has sought to destabilize virtually all of the Middle East and fulfill its mission to destroy the nation of Israel.

The Security Wall Protects Israeli Civilians

GPO/Moshe Milner

Evacuation of Synagogue from Gaza

GPO/Avi Ohayon

Israeli Citizens Protest the Removal of Settlers from Gaza

GPO/Mark Neyman

GPO/Moshe Milner

2001–2010

During this time, the Israel Defense Forces, with the assistance of the United States Defense Department, began the development of a missile defense system that would come to be called the Iron Dome. This system was designed to intercept and destroy missiles and artillery shells fired from Gaza and Southern Lebanon. In subsequent years, the Iron Dome has become a major means of providing greater security for the people of Israel against the terror attacks that the nation had experienced since its formation in 1948.

Despite the constant drumbeat of threats of war and terrorism from the Palestinian Authority and some of Israel's neighbors—most prominently Iran—the Israeli people have refused to allow such threats to impede their progress toward making the Middle East's only democracy into an economic powerhouse that will secure the future of the Israeli people and provide them with resources to maintain the security of the nation.

In the first decade of the twenty-first century, Israel's technology centers experienced dramatic growth as Israeli scientists and technology developers came to be among the most inventive in the world, producing amazing quantum leaps in computer and electronic science and developing a continuing array of inventions that have pushed the world of technology to higher achievements in virtually all fields. In many ways, these advancements have made the lives of Israelis more prosperous, enabling them to enjoy the blessings of life and liberty.

Jerusalem's New Light Rail System

GPO/Moshe Milner

Yokneam High-Tech Center

GPO/Moshe

During this time, the landscape of Israel has undergone significant changes with extensive new highway and road developments, with six freeways and 35 expressways including a superhighway from Jerusalem to Tel Aviv. These transportation arteries have made travel more convenient for Israeli citizens, while, at the same time, providing greater security for the nation. In addition to the new highways, a new passenger rail service in Jerusalem, the *Ha-Rakevet ha-Kala bi-Yerushalayim* (Jerusalem Light Rail), has been added to facilitate transportation in Israel's capital city. Construction began in 2002 and was completed in 2010, with plans for adding lines to other parts of the city.

eisurely Bicycle Ride on the Bulwark of Tel Aviv   Pilgrims Visiting Mount Zion

Hundreds of Israeli Citizens Participate in the Jerusalem Marathon

GPO

Mapping out the Battle Strategy

GPO/Amos Ben Gershom

Israel has continued to encourage the *aliyah* of Jews from around the world as a means of providing security for the global Jewish community in times of increasing antisemitism. A prime example of this welcome was the acceptance of Black Hebrews who had immigrated to Israel and were granted citizenship in 2004. Holocaust survivors from Eastern Europe also continue to be welcomed with open arms to the one safe haven for Jews in the postmodern world: Israel. The nation of Israel has, indeed, become what it was envisioned for centuries to be, a safe and secure homeland for the Jewish people who had been denied that right for nearly two thousand years.

The Jewish people have given such a high priority to education that it has been pursued through the centuries with almost religious fervor. As a statement of the Jewish and Israeli commitment to education, in 2007, the government of Israel made education compulsory for all of its citizens until they reach the age of 18. It has also invested significant amounts of resources in higher education throughout Israel so that the citizenry of this nation are among the most educated in the world. Israel regularly spends upwards of 6% of its Gross Domestic Product on education. As a result, nearly 50% of Israeli citizens hold post-secondary degrees. This achievement is evidence of Israel's perspective that higher education is essential for advanced socioeconomic status for its citizens. This commitment to learning also augments the quality of life in Israel and advances security and peace.

Tanks Preparing for Battle

GPO/Moshe Milner

Iron Dome Missile Defense in Action

GPO/Moshe Milner

Time for Prayer in the Midst of Battle

GPO/Harnik N

Jewish Immigrants Arriving on El Al

Prime Minister Ehud Olmert and US
President George W. Bush

ARROW II INTERCEPTOR
DEVELOPED AND PRODUCED BY MLM
DIVISION OF IAI ELECTRONICS GROUP
• LARGE COVERED AREA
• HYPERSONIC VELOCITY
• HIGH MANEUVERABILITY UTILIZING BOTH
  AERODYNAMICS AND THRUST VECTOR CONTROLS
• TWO HIGH POWER SOLID PROPULSION STAGES
  BOOSTER AND SUSTAINER
• STATE-OF-THE ART DUAL HOMING SENSORS
• ADVANCED NAVIGATION, GUIDANCE AND CONTROL
• POWERFUL FRAGMENTATION WARHEAD
• FAST REACTION TIME

Arrow Missile System

Anti-Missile Defense Facilities

2010–2018
Success and Hope for a Bright Future

The decade that began in 2010 has been an eventful one for the nation of Israel as the nation strides confidently into the twenty-first century with a clear vision of peace, security, and rights for all its citizens. Its solid and well-respected parliamentary democratic form of government provides a voice for all the eight million citizens of the nation and promotes equality among its ethnically and socially diverse people that include over a million non-Jewish citizens.

GPO/Moshe Milner

Jews Making Aliyah Land at Tel Aviv Airport

GPO/Mark Neyman

Celebrating the Festival of Sukkot

Bomb-Destroying Robot

GPO/Sa'ar Ya'acov

Military Graduation Celebration

GPO/Amos Ben Gershom

GPO/Moshe Milner

GPO/ Haim Zach

GPO/ Kobi Gideon

President Shimon Peres Honors IDF Soldiers　　　　**U. S. President Bill Clinton and Israeli President Shimon Peres**

This decade represented the passing of the guard from the generation that had founded the nation of Israel in 1948 to a new generation of leaders. In 2009, President Shimon Peres asked Benjamin Netanyahu to form a government in what must have seemed like a passing of the baton from founders to the new generation. Netanyahu continued to lead efforts to achieve peace through strength.

With the assistance of the United States, Israel deployed and began to operate the air defense system called the "Iron Dome" in Southern Israel and along the Gaza border in 2011. This system helped to minimize the continuing efforts of Hamas to launch missiles into Israel in order to terrorize Israeli civilians and damage Israeli infrastructure.

In 2009, an announcement was made that massive natural gas reserves had been discovered just off the coast of Israel in the Mediterranean Sea. Harnessing this natural asset would prove to be pivotal for the Israeli economy in that it lessened the nation's dependence upon foreign energy sources. This, too, led to greater security in the nation by providing energy resources that cannot be interrupted on the whims of foreign powers.

Helicopters and Ground Crews　　GPO/ Horovitz Doron　　**Lighting the Hanukkah Menorah**　　GPO/ Kobi Gideon

2010–2018

More and more Jews have continued to stream to Israel from nations around the world, especially from Europe, where increasing antisemitism has made life more dangerous and difficult for Jews. The door for *aliyah* remains wide open to all Jews who wish to return to their ancestral homeland where they can experience a degree of security that is not guaranteed in non-Jewish nations.

In 2006, IDF soldier Gilad Shalit was captured by Hamas in a cross-border raid that was launched from one of the tunnels that the terrorist organization had constructed under the Israeli border. Five years later, in a demonstration of the value that the nation of Israel places on the lives of its citizens, the Israeli government was willing to exchange 1,027 Palestinian prisoners who had been collectively responsible for the deaths of some 569 Israeli citizens in exchange for the release of Shalit.

Israel's Famous Merkava Tanks
GPO/Mark Neyman

Inspecting Submarine and Israel's Navy
GPO/Kobi G

Prime Minister Netanyahu Addresses Joint Session of U. S. Congress
GPO/Amos Ben Gershom

Defensive Missile Batteries
GPO

Explosive growth continued during this decade in the fields of science and technology across Israel, as the nation's highly educated and skilled electronics and technology workers continued to be among the world leaders in development of new systems and new applications. Israel now hosts many of the most advanced and powerful technology corporations in the world, and new inventions spring forth from the brain trust of the nation in ever-increasing degrees.

The newest administration in the United States has demonstrated an even higher degree of support for Israel than virtually any of its predecessors. In a conference of more than 50 national leaders from the Arab and Muslim nations of the world in Riyadh, Saudi Arabia, U.S. President Donald J. Trump called for a united front of Middle Eastern nations, including Israel, against the terrorist regimes of Islamic fundamentalists and against the growing threat of Iran. Then, immediately after that conference, President Trump became the first person to fly directly from Riyadh to Tel Aviv. He subsequently visited and prayed at the Western Wall and affirmed the United States' commitment to stand with Israel against all threats to its existence.

The economy of Israel has skyrocketed in the last decade, with outstanding growth, prosperity, and security for the people of Israel. The long and arduous efforts of the previous generations of Israelis have produced fruits that all Israelis can now enjoy. Israel has become self-sufficient because of its astonishing advancements in agronomy and with its development and application of amazing water desalinization technology.

Holocaust Remembrance Day at Yad Vashem
GPO/Amos Ben Gershom

Prime Minister Benjamin Netanyahu GPO

Smoke from a Bombing in the Gaza Strip during Operation Protective Edge

GPO/Kobi Gideon

Without a doubt, the nation of Israel has been blessed by the one who predicted through ancient prophets that the nation that was destroyed by foreign invaders centuries ago would rise again to take the place of honor in the world that the Jewish people have always deserved because of the standards of absolute ethics and social justice For which they collectively stand. The 70 years of history in a sovereign Israel have surely been blessed with wonder after wonder, miracle after miracle, blessing after blessing.

With a government that has an unyielding determination to protect the citizens of Israel at all cost and ensure that the nation not only survives but also thrives, the Israeli people have been freed to focus their considerable determination and vision on making life in Israel free and blessed with peace. Jews from a wide range of cultural and religious backgrounds—from secularists to Ultra-Orthodox—live and work together, striving for the common good of Jews not only in Israel but also around the world. At the same time, they respect the rights of non-Jewish citizens of Israel and the constant stream of visitors from around the world who either make pilgrimage to the Holy Land or reside there for extended periods of time. A free and independent Israel has become the wonder and envy of most of the world.

GPO/Avi Ohayon

Benjamin Netanyahu and U.S. President Donald Trump

Celebrating Passover

GPO/Mark Neyman

Drone Assembly Factory

GPO/Sa'ar Ya'acov

Natural Gas Platform

Benjamin Netanyahu said:
"*There are major moments in the history of Zionism: the Balfour Declaration, the founding of the state, the liberation of Jerusalem and Trump's announcement recognizing Jerusalem as Israel's capital.*"

100 Years in Israel: Growth in Land and Population as Jew

"For I will take you out of the nations; I will

all the countries and bring you back into y

(Ezekiel 36:24)

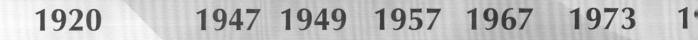

1920   1947 1949 1957 1967 1973 1